Visual Geography Series®

SCOTLAND
...in Pictures

Prepared by
Geography Department

Lerner Publications Company
Minneapolis

Independent Picture Service

**Young Scottish students gather in the courtyard of their
school in central Edinburgh, the Scottish capital city.**

This book is an all-new edition in the Visual Geography Series. Previous editions were published by
Sterling Publishing Company, New York City. The
text, set in 10/12 Century Textbook, is fully revised
and updated, and new photographs, maps, charts, and
captions have been added.

LIBRARY OF CONGRESS CATALOGING-IN-PUBLICATION DATA

Scotland in pictures / prepared by Geography Department,
  Lerner Publications Company.
    p. cm. — (Visual geography series)
    Rev. ed. of: Scotland in pictures / prepared by Donald Grant
Campbell, Irving Nach and others.
    Includes index.
    Summary: Describes the topography, history, society,
economy, and governmental structure of Scotland.
    ISBN 0-8225-1875-9 (lib. bdg.)
    1. Scotland—Juvenile literature. [1. Scotland] I. Campbell,
Donald Grant. Scotland in pictures. II. Lerner Publications
Company. Geography Dept. III. Series: Visual geography
series (Minneapolis, Minn.)
DA762.S32   1991
941.1'0022'2—dc20   90–41726
                                                  CIP
                                                   AC

International Standard Book Number: 0-8225-1975-9
Library of Congress Catalog Card Number: 90–41726

VISUAL GEOGRAPHY SERIES®

Publisher
Harry Jonas Lerner
Associate Publisher
Nancy M. Campbell
Senior Editor
Mary M. Rodgers
Editors
Gretchen Bratvold
Dan Filbin
Photo Researcher
Kerstin Coyle
Editorial/Photo Assistant
Marybeth Campbell
Consultants/Contributors
Barbara Lukermann
Sandra K. Davis
Designer
Jim Simondet
Cartographer
Carol F. Barrett
Indexers
Kristine S. Schubert
Sylvia Timian
Production Manager
Gary J. Hansen

Independent Picture Service

**A lone farmhouse sits amid the uplands of southern Scot-
land.**

Acknowledgments

Title page photo by Bernard Gérard/The Hutchison
Library.

Elevation contours adapted from *The Times Atlas of
the World*, seventh comprehensive edition (New York:
Times Books, 1985).

2 3 4 5 6 7 8 9 10 - JR - 00 99 98 97 96 95

Inverness Castle dominates a hill that overlooks Inverness, a major city in the Highlands of northern Scotland. This castle dates from the 1800s, but a structure has been on the site for more than 1,000 years.

Contents

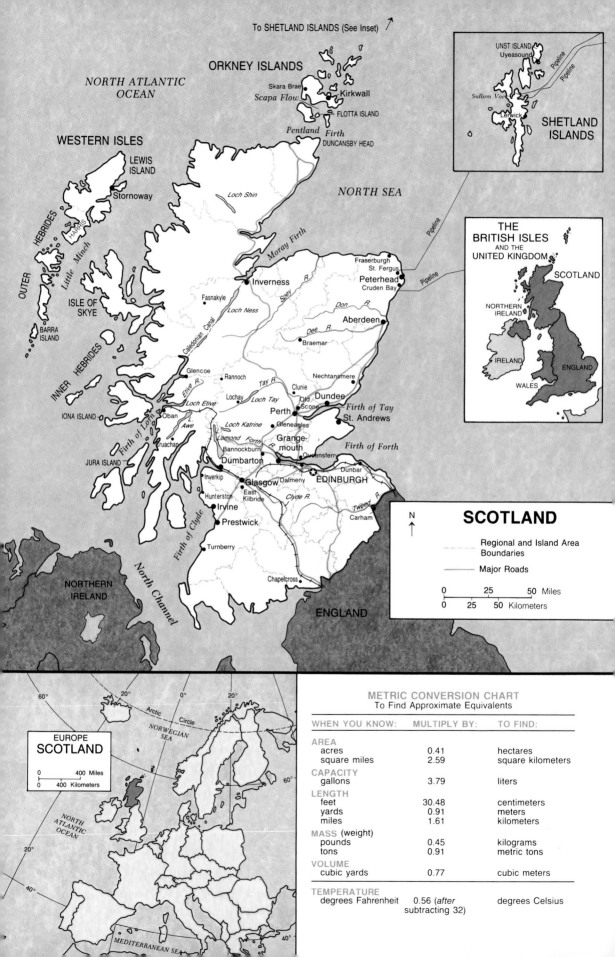

To SHETLAND ISLANDS (See Inset)

NORTH ATLANTIC OCEAN

ORKNEY ISLANDS

Skara Brae
Scapa Flow
Kirkwall
FLOTTA ISLAND

Pentland Firth
DUNCANSBY HEAD

UNST ISLAND
Uyeasound
Pipeline
Pipeline

Sullom Voe
Lerwick

SHETLAND ISLANDS

WESTERN ISLES

LEWIS ISLAND

Stornoway

HEBRIDES
HARRIS

OUTER
Little Minch

ISLE OF SKYE

BARRA ISLAND

INNER HEBRIDES

Loch Shin

NORTH SEA

Moray Firth

Inverness

Fasnakyle
Loch Ness
Caledonian Canal

Spey R.

Fraserburgh
St. Fergus
Peterhead
Cruden Bay

Don R.

Aberdeen

Dee R.
Braemar

IONA ISLAND

Glencoe
Rannoch
Etive R.
Loch Etive
Oban
Awe
L.
Cruachan

Tay R.
Lochay
Loch Tay
Clunie
Old Scone
Perth

Nechtansmere

Dundee
Firth of Tay
St. Andrews

Firth of Lorn

Loch Katrine
Gleneagles
Lomond *Forth*

Dumbarton

JURA ISLAND

Bannockburn

Grange-mouth
Queensferry

Firth of Forth

Inverkip
Glasgow
Dalmeny
EDINBURGH
Dunbar

East Kilbride
Clyde R.

Hunterston
Irvine

Firth of Clyde

Prestwick

Tweed R.
Carham

Turnberry

Chapelcross

NORTHERN IRELAND

North Channel

ENGLAND

THE BRITISH ISLES
AND THE
UNITED KINGDOM

SCOTLAND

NORTHERN IRELAND

IRELAND

ENGLAND

WALES

Pipeline
Pipeline

N

SCOTLAND

- - - Regional and Island Area Boundaries
——— Major Roads

0   25   50 Miles
0   25   50 Kilometers

60°
20°
0°
20°
Arctic Circle
NORWEGIAN SEA

EUROPE
SCOTLAND

0   400 Miles
0   400 Kilometers

NORTH ATLANTIC OCEAN

60°

20°

40°

MEDITERRANEAN SEA
40°

METRIC CONVERSION CHART
To Find Approximate Equivalents

WHEN YOU KNOW:	MULTIPLY BY:	TO FIND:
AREA		
acres	0.41	hectares
square miles	2.59	square kilometers
CAPACITY		
gallons	3.79	liters
LENGTH		
feet	30.48	centimeters
yards	0.91	meters
miles	1.61	kilometers
MASS (weight)		
pounds	0.45	kilograms
tons	0.91	metric tons
VOLUME		
cubic yards	0.77	cubic meters
TEMPERATURE		
degrees Fahrenheit	0.56 (*after* subtracting 32)	degrees Celsius

Wearing bright plaid kilts (pleated skirts), dancers perform during celebrations near the city of Glasgow. Many Scots remain in touch with their heritage through cultural activities, clothing, and language.

Introduction

Scotland is the northernmost country within a European nation called the United Kingdom of Great Britain and Northern Ireland. England, Scotland, and Wales form Great Britain. Northern Ireland covers the northeastern section of the island of Ireland, which lies southwest of Scotland. In 1707 the Act of Union merged England and Wales with Scotland, which had been a separate and independent kingdom until that time.

Settled by Celtic groups from the European continent in about 700 B.C., Scotland has experienced many invasions, including the arrival of the Scotti in the late fifth century A.D. The Scotti, who were Celts from Ireland, not only gave Scotland its name but also introduced their language—Gaelic.

In the succeeding centuries, small communities of people throughout Scotland developed strong family ties. Eventually known as clans, these many groups played an important part in Scotland's history. In the rugged Highlands of northern Scotland were the Highlanders. In southern Scotland lived the Lowlanders, who had more contact with England. For roughly 1,000 years, conflicts between Highlanders and Lowlanders were common.

In addition to its internal disagreements, Scotland was frequently at war

Courtesy of Chevron Corporation

Situated near Scotland's Shetland Islands, this offshore drilling platform is within the Ninian oil field.

of these improvements, some Scots began to question Scotland's union with England. Nationalist groups suggested that oil profits could make Scotland independent of the United Kingdom.

Oil rigs that dot the North Sea were pumping at the peak of their capacity in the mid-1980s. As production started dropping steadily in the late 1980s, many Scots were concerned about what would happen to their economy. In recent years, however, oil fields in the North Sea have been slowly increasing their production again. And while the British government encourages offshore development projects for the present, the challenge will be to balance the availability of natural resources against future needs.

with England. Although the English did not conquer Scotland, they did influence Scottish culture. For example, Scotland gradually adopted the English language. In 1603, after centuries of battling one another, Scotland and England began to cooperate. In that year, a Scottish king, James VI, inherited the English crown.

About a century later, the Act of Union was in effect. Under the act's influence, Scotland developed into a trading and manufacturing hub. By the 1800s, shipbuilding and industry were thriving in the city of Glasgow, which attracted thousands of workers. The new businesses brought prosperity until the 1930s, when a worldwide depression ruined Scotland's economy. Severe unemployment forced many Scots to leave the country in search of jobs. In the following decades, the economic situation in Scotland worsened.

In the 1960s, however, engineers discovered petroleum and natural gas just east of Scotland in the North Sea. These finds lifted Scotland out of its economic slump, providing as many as 100,000 new jobs, and emigration slowed. As a result

Independent Picture Service

A caddie (golf-club carrier) watches as a golfer lightly taps his ball into the hole. Golf has ancient and royal ties to Scotland, and courses exist throughout the country.

Ben Nevis, the tallest peak on the island of Great Britain, rises to 4,406 feet above sea level in Scotland's Grampian Mountains.

1) The Land

Scotland occupies the northern portion of the island of Great Britain, which also includes England and Wales. Great Britain is part of the British Isles, a group of islands off the western coast of the European continent. Scotland's mainland regions and smaller islands together cover 30,414 square miles of territory, making the country about the size of the state of South Carolina.

The North Atlantic Ocean stretches north and west of mainland Scotland. Offshore are the country's three island groups—the Shetlands, the Orkneys, and the Western Isles. The North Channel, an inlet of the North Atlantic, separates southwestern Scotland from Northern Ireland. To the east of Scotland is the North Sea. The Cheviot Hills and the Tweed River in the south form the boundary between Scotland and England.

Topography

Mainland Scotland is divided into three main regions—the Highlands, the Central

Lowlands, and the Southern Uplands. The offshore islands make up a separate topographical unit.

THE MAINLAND

Covering two-thirds of Scotland's territory, the Highlands are a rugged mass of ancient rock. Two parallel mountain ranges—the Grampians and the Northwest Highlands—cut through the region in a southwest-northeast direction. A deep valley known as the Great Glen separates the two mountain systems.

The Grampian Mountains, the country's main range, cover north central Scotland. Ben Nevis (4,406 feet)—the highest peak in the British Isles—rises south of the Great Glen in the Grampians. The other mountain system, the jagged Northwest Highlands, occupies the far north. With a surface of eroded rock, these highlands rise to about 3,000 feet above sea level.

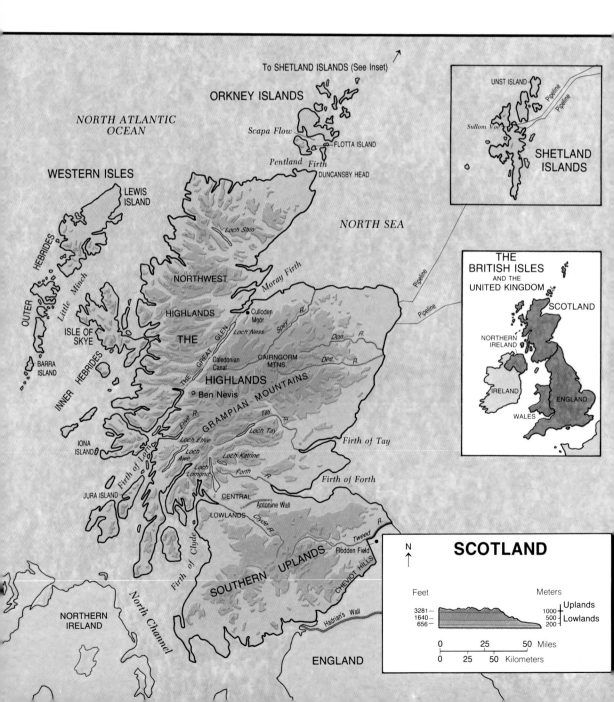

The cliffs of Duncansby Head are the farthest northern extension of mainland Scotland. They face the Pentland Firth (sea inlet), beyond which lie the Orkney Islands.

In addition to glens (valleys) and mountains, the Highlands also contain moorlands (wet, open wildernesses), fast-flowing rivers, and isolated lakes. Because of the rugged terrain, the Highlands are the least populated part of mainland Scotland.

The Central Lowlands form a low-lying belt between the Highlands and the Southern Uplands. The lowlands occupy a narrow valley bounded on both sides by faults (cracks in the earth's crust). Rivers crisscross the Central Lowlands, which account for about 10 percent of Scotland's territory. The region's level terrain and fertile soil have long attracted most of the population. About 75 percent of Scotland's 5.1 million people live in the Central Lowlands. Three of the country's largest cities—Glasgow, Edinburgh, and Dundee —are located in this area.

The rolling countryside of the Southern Uplands includes the Eildon Hills —three peaks that have connections to Scotland's history and legends.

Buried in the sand for hundreds of years, the prehistoric village of Skara Brae on the Orkneys dates from about 2500 B.C. The 10 dwellings, some of which are still beneath sand, suggest what life was like on these islands during the Stone Age.

Although now famous for the oil industry, the Shetlands have long been a farming and herding region. This farmhouse stands near Lerwick, the islands' largest city.

Although a mountainous region, the Southern Uplands are neither as high nor as rugged as the Highlands. Elevated moorlands, a major feature of this area, offer grazing for sheep and cattle. Rough, rocky outcroppings are also part of the landscape. In the far south, the uplands rise to meet the Cheviot Hills along the border with England.

THE ISLANDS

Three main groups of islands are part of Scotland's territory. The Orkneys lie just off the mainland's northern coast, and the Shetlands sit farther to the northeast. The Western Isles, also known as the Hebrides, are located northwest of the Scottish mainland.

The 65 Orkney Islands cover an area of 376 square miles and are irregularly shaped. A low-lying archipelago (group of islands), the Orkneys have fertile soil that supports crops and livestock. Fishing and oil-related industries are also important. Scapa Flow, which was once a British naval base, lies between two of the Orkneys.

Made up of about 100 islands, the wild and rugged Shetlands are the northernmost part of the United Kingdom. The soil on these isolated islands is wet and spongy. Although farmers plant a few crops and raise livestock, fishing and knitware industries have helped the Shetlanders to sustain themselves. The biggest boost to the local economy, however, has been the discovery of oil in the North Sea. Sullom Voe, Europe's largest oil station, was built on one of the Shetlands.

Consisting of more than 500 islands, the Western Isles cover 2,900 square miles of land in the North Atlantic Ocean. The Little Minch, a narrow stretch of water, separates the isles into the Inner and Outer Hebrides. Rocky and wet, the Hebrides support some farming and sheep raising. Fishing and tourism are also major sources of income on this archipelago.

Independent Picture Service

Lying within a few miles of mainland Scotland, the rocky island of Skye is one of the Inner Hebrides.

Photo by Ethel K. MacNeal

Fishermen on Barra—part of the Outer Hebrides—pack freshly caught crabs.

11

Swift-flowing rivers travel throughout Scotland, sometimes emptying into one of the country's many firths. The Etive River crashes over rocks before forming Loch (lake) Etive and entering western Scotland's Firth of Lorn.

Rivers and Lakes

Streams and lakes are found throughout Scotland, offering a resource for hydropower as well as for fishing and irrigation. Some of the waterways empty into estuaries (channels that allow rivers to meet seas) or long bays. Many of the country's bays bear the name *firth*, which is a Scottish Gaelic word meaning "a narrow sea inlet."

Most rivers in Scotland flow eastward to the North Sea. The longest waterway in the country is the Tay, which runs for 120 miles from the Grampian Mountains to the eastern coast. Other rivers that empty into the North Sea include the Tweed, the Forth, the Dee, and the Spey.

Scotland's most important river is the Clyde. It begins in the Southern Uplands and goes northward, spilling over several waterfalls during its 106-mile course. The Clyde River flows past Glasgow, the country's main port, into the Firth of Clyde, an arm of the North Atlantic Ocean.

Scotland has many lakes (called *lochs* in Gaelic), most of which are long and narrow. The largest lake in the country is Loch Lomond, which is located in the Central Lowlands not far from Glasgow. Lochs Tay and Katrine are also in this region. Near the western Grampian Mountains is Loch Awe, and Loch Shin lies within the Northwest Highlands.

An artificial waterway—the Caledonian Canal—spans northern Scotland between the Moray Firth and the Firth of Lorn. To make the 60-mile canal, which parallels the Great Glen, engineers connected the natural lakes with a series of short canals from bay to bay. Loch Ness, a deep lake linked by the canal, is famous for its legendary sea monster.

The 1.5-mile Forth Railway Bridge connects Dalmeny to Queensferry across the Firth of Forth. Accidents killed 56 workers during construction of the elegantly designed bridge, which opened in 1890.

Long, narrow Loch Awe in western Scotland provides water to a hydropower station at Cruachan. Every evening, some of the lake's water is pumped up to a reservoir. During the day, the water flows through electrical generators back to the lake.

Climate

Despite its northern location, Scotland has a mild, moist climate with few extremes in temperature. The North Atlantic Current, which begins in the warm waters of the Caribbean Sea, swirls in from the west. The current warms air masses that move over Scotland, making temperatures mild. Nevertheless, Scotland's inhabitants experience gusty winds, thick fog, and plentiful rainfall throughout the year.

In January, temperatures in the city of Oban on the western coast average about 39° F. Aberdeen, in the east, is a few degrees cooler. In July, readings in Oban hover around 57° F, and those in Aberdeen stay near 56° F. Lerwick—the main city in the Shetlands—has temperatures in those same months of 37° F and 53° F, respectively.

Mountains shield the eastern coast from rain-bearing winds. As a result, this area has the least rainfall—about 25 inches annually. Aberdeen gets roughly 32 inches each year, while Oban receives about 58 inches. More than 40 inches of rain falls

Courtesy of Marybeth Lorbiecki

As snow blankets the ground, a walker climbs Arthur's Seat, a hill in Edinburgh.

Courtesy of Jerry L. McIntyre

The seaside resort of Oban in western Scotland is busy with activity in summer, when the town's mild weather attracts amateur fishermen and scuba divers.

A tough plant that is hard to uproot, the thistle is an important Scottish symbol. Its flowers are usually purple or pink, with prickly leaves. The adoption of the plant as an emblem dates from 1263, when a Scottish king defeated a Norwegian invasion. The attacking army wished to surprise the Scots, but a Norwegian soldier stepped on a thistle and yelled out in pain. His cry alerted the Scots to the Norwegians' position.

Courtesy of British Tourist Authority

on Lerwick per year. The wettest region is the Highlands, where precipitation levels reach about 150 inches. This area gets much of its moisture as snow.

Flora and Fauna

Centuries of farming and settlement have destroyed much of Scotland's native vegetation and animal habitats. Scotland's wildlife enthusiasts and its Forestry Commission have preserved and replanted some of the land. Scotland leads Britain in replanting. The country maintains many scenic areas and has four regional parks.

About 15 percent of Scotland is forested. Northern Scotland contains some Scotch pines that are more than 200 years old. Birches grow near the lochs in the Highlands, where wildflowers and juniper bushes also thrive. Herbs and moor grasses cover western Scotland, and stands of rowan, willow, oak, mountain ash, and pine trees also dot the countryside.

In eastern Scotland, vegetation includes lichen (a mosslike plant) and heather, an evergreen shrub that sprouts purplish flowers in the summer. Scattered clumps of pine, birch, and oak are also common. Southern Scotland, where much of the land has been cleared for farming, contains moorland, oak trees, and birch trees.

Although animal habitats are dwindling, Scotland hosts a variety of mammals. Pine martens (members of the weasel family) feed on many small creatures—from insects to rabbits. The forests provide homes for red deer, foxes, and hares. Some areas of northern Scotland are called "deer forests" because so many red deer inhabit these regions. Each spring, gray seals visit the Orkneys to mate and shed their fur.

15

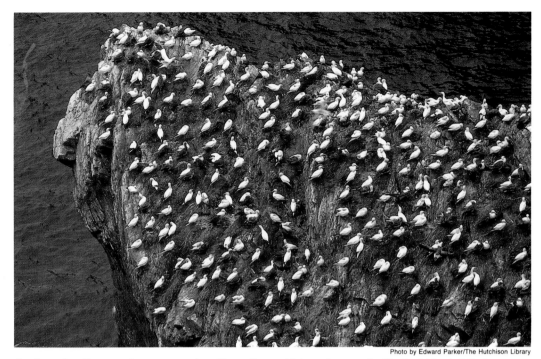

A colony of nesting gannets covers a rock on Herma Ness, a bird sanctuary on the Shetland island of Unst.

Rhododendrons bloom amid the trees and grassy hillsides of central Scotland.

16

Puffins are among the many types of birds that visit and breed in Scotland.

Hundreds of bird species—from the small spotted woodpecker to the graceful osprey—thrive in Scotland. Rugged granite cliffs attract gannets, gulls, and puffins. Decaying Scotch pines offer nesting places for crossbills, whose staple food is pine seeds. At home on the moors or in mountain forests is the golden eagle, one of the world's largest birds of prey. Grouse, which some wealthy people traditionally hunt in late August, are also plentiful in Scotland.

Migrant birds from Iceland and northern Europe stop in Scotland, and geese are particularly abundant at the beginning of winter. Arctic terns, puffins, and kittiwakes breed on the Shetlands. Fewer birds are laying eggs, however, because the islands' natural seafood supplies are dwindling.

Natural Resources

The Central Lowlands contain Scotland's remaining coal reserves, which have been tapped for many decades. The country also has some zinc and silica sand. Since the 1960s, workers have drilled the large reserves of petroleum and natural gas. Income from the sale of these fuels has strengthened the Scottish economy. The main fields lie in the North Sea off the coast of Aberdeen and near the Shetland and Orkney islands.

Scotland's water resources have enabled hydropower and fishing industries to develop. The country contains the largest hydroelectrical facilities in the United Kingdom. Fishermen in small boats and in trawlers ply the waters off Scotland's long and irregular coastline. The country's best fishing grounds exist in eastern and northern waters. The largest hauls are of whitefish, lobster, and mackerel.

Scotland's rushing rivers provide strong sources of hydroelectric power.

Cities

More than 75 percent of Scotland's citizens live in urban areas, mainly in the Central Lowlands. In this region lie Glasgow, Edinburgh, and Dundee. In the northeast is Aberdeen, which has grown in importance and population since the discovery of oil and natural gas.

GLASGOW

Located along the Clyde River in west central Scotland, Glasgow (population 681,000) has long been a major shipbuilding site. Its most rapid growth occurred in the late 1700s, after engineers dredged the Clyde so that large ships could reach the port from the North Atlantic Ocean. In time, Glasgow's excellent harbor handled exports of minerals, tobacco, textiles, automobiles, machinery, whisky, and other manufactured items. In the early 1900s, the city had more than one million people.

Since the mid-twentieth century, urban planners have tried to improve the quality of life for the city's residents, who are called Glaswegians. Slums, known as *gorbals*, were torn down, and new roads and housing were built. Workers scrubbed decades of grime from the city's nineteenth-century buildings as part of a vast program of ur-

Photo by The Hutchison Library

Nineteenth-century housing is a hallmark of Glasgow, Scotland's largest city.

ban renewal. Yet unemployment, especially among young Glaswegians, remains very high as industries close or become outdated. Unemployment and a declining population make the city's economic future uncertain.

Courtesy of Scottish Tourist Board

Diners relax at an outdoor restaurant near Glasgow's George Square.

Despite its many problems, Glasgow has the best overland and air connections of any Scottish urban center. Universities, art museums, and a new exhibition area contribute to the city's strong cultural life.

In fact, the European Community selected Glasgow as the European City of Culture for 1990.

EDINBURGH

Edinburgh (population 442,000), Scotland's capital, lies on the country's eastern coast along the Firth of Forth. Founded in the seventh century, the city has long been a hub of Scottish culture and education. Dominating Edinburgh is its eleventh-century castle, where military pageants often take place. The castle overlooks Princes Street, the main thoroughfare. Another group of streets—collectively called the Royal Mile—leads to Holyroodhouse, a royal residence.

Although Edinburgh has art museums, historical buildings, and fine schools, its major cultural attraction is the Edinburgh International Festival. Held each August, this celebration of music, drama, and film brings performers and spectators from many nations to Scotland's capital.

The city's major businesses include printing and publishing firms, financial institutions, and insurance companies. Within and near the capital are many breweries, distilleries, paper mills, and clothing factories. Edinburgh's shipping facilities export fertilizers, textiles, and beverages.

Courtesy of John Rice

On a clear day, the view of Edinburgh includes a broad stretch of the capital and beyond it the Firth of Forth.

The site of a seventh-century stronghold, Edinburgh Castle dominates the city and has been a residence, a fort, and a prison.

Courtesy of British Tourist Authority

19

ABERDEEN AND DUNDEE

With a population of 281,000, Aberdeen is Scotland's third largest urban center. Located at the mouths of the Dee and Don rivers along the North Sea, the city is the main farming and industrial hub for northern Scotland. Although Aberdeen has long been a major shipping center and fishing port, it has expanded in recent years because of the petroleum finds in the North Sea. In addition to oil products, Aberdeen's factories manufacture paper, food, chemicals, and textiles. Many of the city's buildings are made of a locally cut pink granite, which gives Aberdeen a distinctive appearance.

Dundee (population 170,000) lies on the Firth of Tay along the east central coast. Although an ancient trading city, Dundee became more prosperous in the 1800s, when its docks handled a huge volume of products made from jute (a fibrous plant). In the modern era, Dundee is a shipbuilding and manufacturing center that exports locally produced computers, candy, jams, tires, and jewelry. Cargo vessels bring shipments of oil to Dundee from the North Sea.

Although now noted as an oil center, Aberdeen is also a centuries-old fishing hub on Scotland's eastern coast.

Courtesy of British Tourist Authority

Dating from about the first century B.C., the Broch (round tower) of Gurness is one of the finest ancient remains on the Orkney Islands. Located on the windy coast, the broch once had a narrow, guarded passageway that led to several rooms.

2) History and Government

Thousands of years ago, during the last Ice Age, a low-lying land bridge connected the British Isles to the European mainland. In time, the sheets of ice that covered the land began to melt and flooded the land bridge. By about 6000 B.C., Great Britain had become an island.

Early Inhabitants

Historians believe that Scotland's first inhabitants reached the region in about 6000 B.C. The earliest peoples came from Europe by sea. By about 4500 B.C., another migration from the continent had occurred. The newcomers knew farming and were also experienced fishermen and herders. Skilled carvers of stone, these peoples shaped the material into weapons and tools. They built large burial chambers, called cairns, for their dead.

In about 2500 B.C., peoples who used copper and bronze arrived in Scotland. They were also farmers and herders and had a unique way of burying their dead. These peoples placed the corpse in a cramped position in a small tomb along with weapons and decorative drinking cups, known as beakers. Evidence of these so-called Beaker folk exists in western Scotland. The Beaker folk taught local inhabitants to use bronze. Between 2000 and

700 B.C., bronze became the preferred material for making broad swords and heavy axes.

During these centuries—which historians have termed the Bronze Age—Scotland's peoples had little contact with outsiders. In about 700 B.C., however, raiding groups from Europe—called Celts—began coming to Scotland in search of animal hides and fish. A warlike people who used iron weapons, the Celts soon conquered the country. They established extended family units that fought one another for power.

By the first century A.D., the Celts in Scotland had become experienced iron-workers and boatbuilders. They crafted fancy jewelry, strong weapons, and fine pottery. Farmers made good use of the available fertile land. Although no single group ruled the others, the northern Celts were stronger than the southern Celts.

The Roman Era

During the first century A.D., armies from the Roman Empire, which was centered in what is now Italy, invaded England and Wales. Scotland escaped the initial Roman attacks. By about A.D. 80, however, the Romans had conquered England, which they called Britannia, and were turning their attention to northern Great Britain.

Heading the invasion of Scotland was Gnaeus Julius Agricola, a young Roman officer. By A.D. 83, Agricola and his soldiers were ready to fight the northern Celts, whom the Romans at first called Caledonians. The next year, in a major battle at Mons Graupius, Agricola's army defeated the large Caledonian forces.

From their defeat, the Caledonians realized that they could not attack the Roman army directly. Instead, the Celts chose to raid and harass the invaders. These tactics worked, and by A.D. 122 the Roman border had retreated as far south as the Cheviot Hills. In that year, the Roman emperor Hadrian visited the region and ordered the army to build a wall to seal off Britannia from the Caledonians. Parts of this 73-mile barrier—called Hadrian's Wall—still stand in northern England.

The raids on Roman-occupied lands continued, however, and by the A.D. 140s the Romans had constructed another defensive barricade. Located north of Hadrian's Wall, this divider—named the Antonine Wall after a new emperor—stretched from the Firth of Forth to the Firth of Clyde. Despite this show of Roman power, the

Hadrian's Wall is situated in the far north of England, which lies south of Scotland. During the second century A.D., when England was under the control of the Romans, the Roman army built the long wall to keep Celtic raiders out of England.

Geometric tattoos and sturdy weapons distinguished the hardy Scottish warriors called Picts.

Caledonians kept up their swift attacks. By the A.D. 300s, the Caledonians dominated the country. Because of unique tattoos that the Caledonians wore on their bodies, they became known as Picts, meaning "painted" in Latin, the language of the Romans.

Dramatic changes took place within the Roman Empire in the late fourth century, when high-ranking commanders and nobles began to compete for power. Units of the Roman army left Britannia to protect other parts of the empire. By the early fifth century, Rome had abandoned its lands on the British Isles.

Invasions, Christianity, and the Clans

As Roman control weakened, the Picts invaded northern England. In the late fifth century, Angles and Saxons—Germanic peoples from northern Europe—began to attack southern Scotland. At about the same time, Irish Celts, called Scotti, raided Pictish settlements. These invasions helped to unify the Picts, who had become the strongest Celtic group in Scotland by the early sixth century.

The Picts occupied all of the Highlands and most of eastern Scotland. Near Oban, the Scotti formed the kingdom of Dalriada, which included the islands of Jura and Iona. Celtic Britons from the south took over lands that eventually became known as Strathclyde. The invading Angles conquered territory in the southeast and named the region Lothian.

These groups regularly fought each other for land and cattle—the main forms of wealth at that time. Amid the warfare, Celts from Ireland made a strong attempt to bring the Christian religion to the people in this rugged territory. An Irish monk

A carved stone slab from the Antonine Wall—a Roman-built barrier in central Scotland—shows a Roman horseman trampling several Pictish soldiers.

23

Columba, a monk from Ireland, introduced the inhabitants of Scotland to Christianity in the A.D. 500s. According to legend, he won the confidence of a powerful local leader, who gave Columba the land on which he founded his monastery.

Photo by Mansell Collection

named Columba led a missionary expedition in A.D. 563, setting up a monastery on Iona.

For more than 30 years, Columba and his missionaries traveled through Dalriada, Pictland, and Strathclyde to convert the Celts. By the time of Columba's death in 597, Christianity had taken firm root among the various Celtic peoples and their leaders. Converting the Angles to Christianity became the challenge of a separate missionary expedition. By the seventh century, the Angles had also accepted the Christian faith.

Although Christianity became a common bond among Scotland's peoples, their warlike way of life continued. The stronghold of Celtic traditions lay in the Highlands, where family loyalty was very important.

Heading each extended family—or clan—was a male chieftain. He led male clan members in battle and had the right to claim their property. In recognition of a chieftain's authority, clan members adopted the name of their leader, adding the prefix *Mac* or *Mc* (meaning "son of") to signify kinship.

Fight for Unity

Over several hundred years, the balance of power shifted among the four groups that controlled what is now Scotland. The Picts defeated the Angles at Nechtansmere in 685. This victory prevented Anglo-Saxon expansion, although Lothian—and its main city of Edinburgh—continued to exist on the eastern coast.

Beginning in the late eighth century, raiders from Norway, called Vikings, began to attack the coasts and islands of Scotland. They sacked the monastery at Iona in about 795 and destroyed other settlements on the mainland. By the mid-800s, the Vikings had taken over the Orkneys and the Shetlands. The invaders set up military outposts from which they could safely attack the northern mainland.

The Viking sieges, which reached their height in the ninth century, weakened the Picts. As a result, the king of the Scotti, Kenneth MacAlpin, was able to conquer Pictland in 843. King Kenneth combined Scotia and Pictland for the first time, forming a Scottish realm called Alba. He moved a sacred rock named the Stone of Destiny to the Pictish capital of Scone. A symbol of royal authority, the rock became known as the Stone of Scone.

King Kenneth arranged for his daughter to marry the ruler of Strathclyde, thus giving Alba a claim to Strathclyde's throne. Strathclyde was continually under attack from the Vikings, who destroyed Dumbarton, Strathclyde's capital city, in 870. Despite these invasions, Strathclyde survived as a separate political unit with family ties to Alba.

UNITY ACHIEVED

Through these events, Alba became the region's strongest kingdom, and its

By the sixth century, four main groups—the Picts, the Scotti, the Britons, and the Angles—occupied parts of what is now mainland Scotland. The Vikings held outlying islands. Gradually, the four mainland peoples intermarried or conquered one another, so that by the eleventh century, Scotland was a unified country.

Artwork by Laura Westlund

immediate goal was to limit the power of the Vikings. In the late ninth century, the Vikings were well established on the Orkneys the Shetlands, and the Western Isles. Skilled farmers as well as experienced sailors, the Vikings had also settled parts of the Highlands.

The growing strength of the southern Anglo-Saxon kingdoms—which had formed a single realm called England—was also of concern to Alba. Possessing greater wealth and superior weapons, the English forced the Scottish kings to recognize England's monarch as overlord (supreme ruler) in the tenth century.

Despite this humiliation, Alba's rulers fought the English, as well as other groups, to build up the Scottish kingdom. At the Battle of Carham in 1018, the Scottish king Malcolm II brought Lothian in the southeast under his authority. In the same year, Malcolm's grandson and heir, Duncan, inherited the kingdom of Strathclyde in the southwest. By 1034, when Duncan succeeded his grandfather, he had united the various kingdoms into one realm called Scotland. Its citizens became known as Scots.

Norman Influence

In 1066 armies from Normandy (now part of France) seized England. Poorer than England, Scotland did not seem like a worthy conquest to the Normans. Instead, they were content to force the Scottish king, Malcolm III, to accept the Norman ruler of England as overlord.

The interaction between Scotland and England included language and cultural influences. In southern Scotland, English became the common tongue, although people in the north continued to use Scottish Gaelic. Children of the Scottish royal family were educated in England. These internal changes occurred alongside improvements in farming and trade that were also happening in Norman-ruled England. On Scotland's grassy hillsides, farmers began to raise large flocks of sheep. These herds provided wool to a growing export industry.

As a result of Scotland's close ties with England, the Scottish king David I introduced many Norman ideas after he inherited Scotland's crown in 1124. Educated at the English court, David gave estates in southern Scotland to many of his Norman-English friends. He set up a

Courtesy of John Rice

At Kirkwall on the Orkneys stands St. Magnus Cathedral. It was built in the Anglo-Norman style that came from Norman-ruled England. Beneath the cathedral's foundation are the bones of Saint Magnus. He was killed in 1116, when his cousin, a Norwegian earl, fought Magnus for control of the islands. For many centuries, the cathedral was under the authority of bishops in Trondheim, Norway.

Norman-style government, which awarded lands in exchange for loyalty, money, and service. The king designed many abbeys in the Norman fashion, and he issued the first Scottish coins.

The kingdom's strongest support lay among the people of the lowland areas of the south. Although the north was officially governed by Scotland's laws, it actually was under the control of the clans, who followed ancient customs. Poor overland connections between the north and the south enabled the Highlanders to rule themselves.

Progress and Strife

In the 1200s, Scotland developed a governmental structure. Powerful Scottish landowners and some wealthy merchants began to advise the king, and these groups eventually formed the Scottish Parliament. To rid the kingdom of the Norwegians—who controlled the Hebrides, Orkneys, and Shetlands—the Scottish king Alexander III pushed back a fleet of Norwegian ships in 1263. His victory brought the Hebrides under Scottish control.

This progress was seriously endangered when both Alexander and his heir died within a few years of each other. Their deaths left the succession open to several high-born people. Among the contenders were Robert Bruce and John Baliol.

In 1291 Scotland's noble families asked the English monarch, Edward I, to oversee the fair selection of the next Scottish king. Edward was not an impartial judge, however. He had recently taken over Wales and intended to seize Scotland. Edward chose Baliol, whom Edward believed he could control.

As Scotland's ruler, however, Bailol resisted Edward's authority. The Scottish king allied his country with France, England's traditional rival. In response, Edward invaded Scotland in 1296, capturing Edinburgh and stealing the sacred Stone of Scone. Baliol gave up the throne after

Courtesy of Dean and Chapter of Westminster

In 1296, during one of the many wars between Scotland and England, the English king Edward I captured Scotland's sacred Stone of Scone. Upon it, Scottish kings were crowned. Edward ordered a new coronation chair to be built to enclose the stone. Since 1308 English monarchs have been crowned in this chair, with the sacred stone tucked under the seat.

a defeat at Dunbar, and many Scottish nobles had to swear loyalty to Edward. The English king put his own officials in charge of the Scottish government and stationed English troops throughout the country.

These harsh measures provoked the Scots to act. A minor landowner named William Wallace led a grass-roots rebellion among the Scottish common people. Lacking the support of the Scottish nobles, however, Wallace eventually lost in battle to the English, who executed him in 1305.

Robert Bruce, the grandson of Baliol's rival, also fought to rid Scotland of the English. In 1306 he went to Scone, where he claimed the kingship. A talented commander, Bruce transformed the Scottish troops from a disorganized army into a skilled fighting force. In the meantime,

In 1314 the Scottish soldier and king Robert Bruce instructed his troops before the Battle of Bannockburn. The victory of the Scots over the English eventually led England to recognize Scotland's independence.

Edward I died and left the crown to his son, Edward II, who lacked his father's military experience.

After several years of harassing the English, the Scottish troops won a decisive victory at the Battle of Bannockburn in 1314. In 1320 Scotland declared itself completely independent of England, but the war dragged on until 1328. In that year, Edward II's successor agreed to Scotland's declaration and recognized Bruce as King Robert I.

Monarchs and Clans

For Scotland, the fourteenth through the sixteenth centuries were a time of internal fighting as well as conflicts with England. Many of King Robert's successors inher-

ited the throne as children. They ruled with the help of regents—adult relatives who supervised and protected the young monarchs. The heads of powerful clans gained influence during this period of political uncertainty.

Ordinary citizens struggled through these years of war, which had destroyed fields and had weakened the wool trade. The population rose and fell as warfare and the Black Death (a deadly disease) eliminated entire communities. For the survivors, Scotland remained a poor country where the main sources of wealth were cattle and sheep.

In 1371, after being regent for many years, Bruce's grandson Robert Stewart inherited the throne and founded the House of Stewart (later spelled Stuart).

Independent Picture Service

Dunvegan Castle on the island of Skye has been the home of the MacLeod clan since the thirteenth century. Powerful extended families, the clans once wielded absolute authority in many parts of Scotland.

Photo by Mansell Collection

Although to outsiders Scotland seemed a wild and warlike place, its monarchs were often well educated and diplomatic. James I, who reigned from 1406 to 1437, was a gifted poet who composed *The Kingis Quair,* a long poem in the Scots language. He also confronted the leaders of the strongest clans to assert his own authority.

Members of this family ruled Scotland for more than 300 years.

Many of the Stuart rulers died violently. For example, Robert's grandson, James I, was assassinated in 1437 after he tried to assert royal authority against the clans and lowland nobles. James I's grandson, James III, was also assassinated. Before he was killed, he acquired the remaining areas of present-day Scotland—the Orkneys and the Shetlands—by marrying the daughter of the king of Denmark and Norway in 1472. James III's son, James IV, died in warfare against the English at Flodden Field in 1513.

In an effort to improve relations with England, James IV had married Margaret Tudor, the daughter of England's King Henry VII. After her husband was killed, Margaret tried to protect the inheritance of her young son, James V, by acting as his regent. Proclaimed old enough to rule in 1524, James V introduced reforms to limit the power of the nobles. He also waged war against England, which was again trying to control Scotland. Wounded in battle in 1542, he died soon afterward, leaving a week-old daughter named Mary to succeed him.

James V's death occurred at a time when much of Europe was undergoing a religious change called the Protestant Reformation. This widespread movement challenged the authority of Roman Catholicism, which had been the only religion in Scotland since the sixth century. England had already established its own Protestant church. Many Scots believed that the reforms taking place in England and on the continent should also come to Scotland.

Mary, Queen of Scots

During these religious shifts, Queen Mary—a devout Roman Catholic—went to France to marry the heir to the French throne. Her French-Catholic mother, who acted as regent, became involved in the disagreements between Scotland's pro-English Protestants and pro-French Catholics. With the help of Elizabeth Tudor, the Protestant queen of England, Scottish Protestants took over the Scottish government in 1560. Led by an energetic, strong-willed preacher named John Knox, the new Parliament named the Protestant faith as Scotland's national religion.

Widowed at 17, Mary returned to her homeland in 1561 to take up her duties as queen of Scotland. She also felt she had a legal claim to the English throne through her Tudor grandmother. Mary's family ties made her a threat to Elizabeth. The Scottish queen's Catholic faith put her in conflict with her people, most of whom favored the Presbyterian sect of Protestantism.

Catholic-Protestant tensions remained high throughout Mary's reign. In 1565 she married her Catholic cousin and gave birth to a son the next year. After being captured by Protestant forces in 1567, Mary gave up her throne. Her infant son—whom

guardians were raising as a Protestant—succeeded her as James VI. Mary escaped to England.

Suspecting the former Scottish queen of plotting to overthrow her, Elizabeth imprisoned Mary and eventually executed her in 1587. Just before Elizabeth died in 1603, she named her Protestant cousin, King James VI of Scotland, as her successor. He chose to rule the two kingdoms separately and thus also became James I of England. The two realms—which had warred against one another for so many centuries—now had one leader. James and his family moved to London, the English capital city.

Religious Conflicts

Although a committed Protestant, James disliked the strict Presbyterian sect. It favored an independent, elected community —instead of bishops and priests appointed

A portrait at Blair Castle in east central Scotland shows Mary, Queen of Scots, and her son, James VI. Mary did not raise her son. In fact, she was forced to give up her throne to him when he was a year old and never saw him again. He reigned as king of Scotland from 1567 until 1603, when—through his English cousin Queen Elizabeth—he inherited England's crown as well.

by the monarch—to run the church. Nevertheless, by the seventeenth century, the Presbyterian Church of Scotland was well established. It had popular support because of its emphasis on equality and education.

Unlike his ancestors, who ruled Scotland in person and by force, James VI governed his Scottish kingdom from London and with a pen. He wrote to the Scottish Parliament, telling it what goals he wanted its members to accomplish. James left much of the work of governing to local administrators and visited Scotland only once before his death in 1625.

This remote way of dealing with Parliament was also used by James's son, Charles I, who knew little of the northern kingdom's traditions. Uncomfortable with the independence of Presbyterianism, the new king sought to make the Church of Scotland similar to the Church of England (also called the Anglican Church).

Riots erupted in Scotland in the late 1630s, when Charles tried to introduce an Anglican prayerbook into Presbyterian church services. A group of Presbyterian nobles, merchants, and ministers drew up a counterproposal called the National Covenant. By the 1640s, the Covenanters were insisting that the national government and the monarch fully accept Presbyterianism. Their demands led to armed conflict between the Covenanters and the king's troops.

The English Parliament was also dissatisfied with Charles's approach to governing. Civil war broke out in England between the Royalists, who supported the king, and the Parliamentarians, who backed Parliament. A strong force among the Parliamentarians was the Puritans, a strict group of English Protestants. After war broke out, Charles went to Scotland. By 1646 the king had surrendered to the Covenanters. These Presbyterians released the king to the Puritans, who were supposed to persuade Charles I to change his ways. Instead, the Puritans beheaded him in 1649 after a public trial.

Although the monarch of Scotland was now also the ruler of England, the two kingdoms were governed separately. Charles II, who survived the English civil wars of the 1640s, claimed the Scottish kingdom in 1650 but was unable to assert his rights to England until 1660.

THREATS TO PRESBYTERIANISM

Shocked by the execution of their king, the Covenanters initially supported his son and successor, Charles II, who had agreed to the National Covenant. But after the Puritans defeated the Scots in three important battles, Scotland was too weak to remain independent of England. Charles fled to the European continent, and the Puritan leader, Oliver Cromwell, took over the Scottish government.

In 1658 Cromwell died, and his government survived only until 1660. In that year, the English and Scottish Parliaments offered the crown to Charles II, who then returned to England. He did not visit Scotland during this part of his reign. Instead, he ruled the country from England through a council in Edinburgh.

Seventeenth-century coins depict James VII *(left)* and William and Mary *(right)* who vied for control of Scotland in the late 1600s.

The Presbyterians expected the new king to uphold the National Covenant. But Charles appointed bishops and priests to run the Scottish church, instead of allowing Presbyterians to hold elections to the ruling posts. Rebellions brewed over this religious issue in the 1670s and 1680s. Tensions increased in 1685, when Charles died and his Roman Catholic brother inherited the crown. The new king, James VII, intended to make Scotland a Roman Catholic country.

ROYAL CONFLICTS

Within four years, however, the English Parliament had removed James from the English throne because of his Catholic views. His Protestant son-in-law and daughter, William and Mary, became king and queen of England. In Scotland, many Catholic Highlanders still supported James VII as king of Scotland. These people came to be called Jacobites, after the Latin word for James.

The issue led to warfare between the Highlanders and government troops. When the Highlanders lost, James fled to France, where he and his second wife raised their young son. In the meantime, the Scottish Parliament had accepted William as king

of Scotland. In 1690 he agreed to a law that established the Church of Scotland under a Presbyterian system.

Clans in the Highlands continued to oppose the Protestant king. William decided to make an example of Alexander MacIan MacDonald of Glencoe. He was the last chieftain to announce his support for William. After several days of accepting MacDonald's hospitality, a small force sent by the king murdered MacDonald's entire family. The Glencoe Massacre of 1692 lost William the support of many Highlanders. The king also offended the Lowlanders by adopting policies that severely limited Scotland's foreign trade.

Union with England

In this negative atmosphere, the issue of the formal union of Scotland and England arose. The idea met fierce resistance in Scotland because most Scots believed their country would have an inferior status in the union. But those in favor of forming one kingdom pointed out the opportunities for free trade with England and with England's colonies. They also insisted that Scotland's laws and religious system would not change.

Photo by Mansell Collection

In 1692 King William ordered British soldiers to kill members of the clan of Alexander MacIan MacDonald of Glencoe, including his wife, children, and tenant farmers. By this show of power, William hoped to intimidate any Scots who might still support James VII as king.

William died in 1702, and Anne Stuart, the last Protestant child of James VII, inherited the throne. One of the reasons England favored union with Scotland was that Queen Anne had no direct heir. The English government wanted Anne's Protestant cousin in Germany to succeed her. James VII's Catholic son, James Stuart, was Anne's half-brother. He still lived in France and considered himself the rightful king. Most Scots and English believed that if James Stuart became king, civil war would break out between Catholics and Protestants.

In the early 1700s, both Parliaments hotly debated a plan for union. Under the terms of the plan—called the Act of Union—Scotland would retain its legal system and independent church. Scotland would no longer have its own Parliament, however, and would send its delegates to sessions in London.

The two Parliaments eventually passed the Act of Union, which took effect in 1707. It created a new nation called the United Kingdom of Great Britain (also called Britain), with one Parliament and one monarch. By this time, political parties had formed. Most Scottish members of Parliament were Tories and favored the existing policies of the government. The opposition group, known as the Whigs, wanted to reduce the power of the monarchy.

JACOBITE REBELLIONS

Anne died in 1714, and the next year the Jacobites proclaimed James Stuart as James VIII of Scotland. The British Parliament had already named a German prince, George of Hanover, as king of

Photo by Mansell Collection

In 1707 the Act of Union formally merged Scotland and England. Here, Queen Anne listens as an official reads the act.

33

Prince Charles Edward Stuart was often called Bonnie Prince Charlie because of his youth and physical beauty. In the 1740s, he championed his family's attempts to retake the Scottish throne.

Great Britain. The Jacobites and government troops fought several battles, and by 1716 King George's soldiers had restored order in Scotland. The Jacobite leaders were executed, or exiled, or stripped of their weapons. Antigovernment feelings persisted, however, and another Jacobite rebellion occurred in 1745.

By this time, James Stuart was an old man. His young son Charles Edward—popularly known as Bonnie Prince Charlie—came from France to put the Stuarts back on the throne. Jacobite clans rushed to his support, and Charles Edward's father was again proclaimed king of Scotland. Meanwhile, the government gathered troops to fight the Jacobites. The two groups finally clashed at Culloden Moor in 1746, and the prince's outnumbered forces scattered and were defeated. Charles Edward fled to the Hebrides and then sailed for France.

The British government executed or imprisoned supporters of the second Jacobite rebellion, and the property of the rebels was seized or burned. Highland clans were forbidden to wear kilts—the traditional

Kilted clansmen litter the field as Prince Charles Edward rallies his supporters at the Battle of Culloden in 1745. After British troops defeated the prince's army, the Stuarts did not maintain their claim to Scotland's throne.

clothing of Scottish warriors. They could not own weapons, and the bagpipe, a musical instrument used at clan gatherings, was banned.

The Industrial Revolution

These measures weakened the clan system. In its place came government management of lands in the Highlands. The new arrangement brought improvements in industry and agriculture. These changes —part of a nationwide transformation known as the Industrial Revolution—were also happening in other areas of the United Kingdom.

Scotland's textile industry switched from weaving wool to making linen, cotton, and jute products. Landowners in central Scotland hired workers to dig coal on their estates. The coal was used as fuel for new machines and furnaces. Engineers dredged the Clyde River in the 1770s, enabling larger ships to reach Glasgow. Investors built ironworks and shipyards in the city.

Many Scots played important roles in this national transformation. James Watt, for example, improved steam engines that powered many kinds of machines. Thomas Telford, once a stonemason, built bridges, highways, and canals throughout Great Britain. Among his engineering feats was the Caledonian Canal, which opened in 1822.

Farm workers from all over Scotland streamed to the industrial cities of Glasgow, Edinburgh, Dundee, and Perth to take mining and factory jobs. Many of these new arrivals had been pushed off their land under a system of "clearances." This arrangement allowed landowners to evict their tenant farmers, called crofters, to combine the small parcels of farmland into vast estates.

POLITICAL REFORMS AND SHIFTS

Although mine owners and factory managers were making large amounts of

Courtesy of Library of Congress

Born near Glasgow in 1736, James Watt was trained to make technical instruments. For many years, he worked at the University of Glasgow, where he improved several instruments and machines. Although Watt did not invent the steam engine, he made it run more efficiently. This improvement allowed steam engines to be widely used as a form of mechanical power. Watt patented (claimed legal right to) his designs, which others had to pay him to use. He died a wealthy man in 1819. For his contribution to engineering, scientists gave the name *watt* to the unit of power that produces or uses energy.

money, the standard of living for the workers was poor. Wages were low, and laborers, including young children, toiled in unhealthy and dangerous conditions. Most workers lived in crowded slums, where diseases such as cholera were common. Many young Scots left their homeland for the United States or for Britain's colonies to escape the squalid living conditions in Scotland.

By the 1830s, Parliament had become aware of these problems. It passed a reform bill that limited work hours and that gave more men the right to vote. In the mid-1800s, laborers throughout the nation pressed for more reforms. Their efforts resulted in a public health act, a national educational system, and voting rights for workers. These changes fostered political shifts, and new parties formed. The Tories evolved into the Conservative party, and the Whigs became the Liberal party.

Keir Hardie *(speaking center),* **the founder of the Scottish Labour party, merged his organization with a similar group working in England. The Labour party now holds most of the Scottish legislative seats in the British Parliament.**

Photo by Bettmann Archive

CHANGES OF THE LATE 1800s

The Industrial Revolution made the United Kingdom the world's biggest trader in the late 1800s. The British navy protected the sea-lanes on which trade depended, and wealth poured into the kingdom. Scottish politicians helped to govern this growing commercial empire, and Scottish soldiers played a part in defending it from rival powers.

Meanwhile, a Scot named Keir Hardie founded the Scottish Labour party in 1888 to represent the interests of the working class. Some of the party's goals, such as nationalization (transferring private property to state ownership), were far different from the aims of the Liberals and the Conservatives. The Labour party found supporters among dissatisfied workers in Glasgow and Edinburgh. In 1900 Keir Hardie became the first Labour candidate to take a seat in Parliament.

During this period, Britain made international alliances to maintain its control of world markets and its power in Europe. Competing with Britain was Germany, which had rapidly industrialized and improved its military strength.

World Wars and Economic Decline

By 1914 Germany was Britain's main rival for economic and political influence in the world. In that year, Germany's ally Austria attacked Serbia in eastern Europe. Because of the United Kingdom's military agreements, this action brought Britain and its allies into World War I. Thousands of Scots enlisted or were drafted to fight in the global conflict. The British navy sent its fleet to Scapa Flow—its base in the Orkneys. From there, British ships engaged German boats in an ongoing naval war.

At first, the world war had public support. But, after four years of indecisive battles with many casualties, popular backing weakened. By 1918, when Britain and its allies finally defeated Germany, the United Kingdom had lost 800,000 people.

After the war, returning Scottish soldiers expected to share in the prosperity of peacetime. Their expectations were not met, however, because Scotland's industrial sector declined in the 1920s. In the 1930s, a worldwide economic depression occurred. Large numbers of northern factories closed, and in Glasgow the

In the misty climate of Scapa Flow, ships stand at anchor during World War I (1914–1918).

In 1935 cars and people on foot crossed a new bridge that was the last link in a road from Glasgow to Inverness. Public-works projects, such as road building, were part of the British government's efforts to improve Scotland's economy in the 1930s.

unemployment rate reached more than 60 percent. Again many Scots left their homeland in search of better conditions. As economic troubles persisted, support grew for the Labour party and for a home-rule movement. The movement's members wanted Scotland to govern itself.

In 1928, in response to agitation for home rule, the government gave the secretary of state for Scotland more power and made the secretary a member of the ruling British cabinet. The secretary's main office was in Edinburgh, rather than in London. In the same year, the Scottish National party was founded, and its platform called for a separate legislature to handle Scottish affairs.

Events in Europe interrupted the home-rule movement. In 1939 Germany invaded Poland, and Britain's alliances again brought the kingdom into a global conflict. Scottish men and women enlisted, or they worked in factories to support the United Kingdom during World War II. German planes bombed Glasgow and its surroundings, but the rest of Scotland remained largely untouched. Scapa Flow again became a base for Britain's naval fleet, and many soldiers trained in the Highlands.

By 1943 Britain and its allies began to win the war, and in 1945 Germany surrendered. Many Scots feared that the severe unemployment of the 1920s and 1930s would return in the postwar period. The Labour party won the elections in 1945, and the new government enacted programs that broadened the role of the secretary of state for Scotland. The Labourites also passed legislation that gave all Britain's citizens low-cost medical services and that put major industries under state control.

The Modern Era

By the 1950s, these new policies had created jobs, and the earnings of Scottish people had risen. For the first time, many could afford to own their homes and to buy cars. In the same period, Scottish nationalists called for a separate legislature.

In the 1960s, British and foreign engineers began to look for natural gas in the North Sea. The explorers not only found the expected deposits but also discovered

In 1942, during World War II, Scottish recruits practiced maneuvers near Invergary. Rugged areas of Scotland often were the training ground for new soldiers.

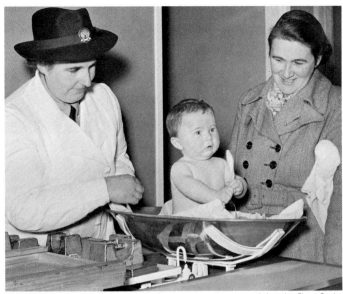

In the 1950s, the National Health Service provided free or very affordable medical care to the people of Scotland. Here, a nurse weighs a five-month-old boy in an Edinburgh clinic.

substantial fields of petroleum. These supplies lay closest to Scotland, mainly near the Shetlands and the Orkneys. Private companies set up drilling rigs, and pipelines carried fuels to the mainland. Jobs multiplied as Aberdeen and the two island areas became the hub of a new economic activity.

Many members of the Scottish National party (SNP) suggested that these deposits could make Scotland economically independent of England. This prospect renewed interest in home rule in the 1960s and 1970s. The first SNP member, Winifred Ewing, took her seat in the British Parliament in 1967. Other SNP delegates

Discoveries of oil and natural gas in the North Sea in the 1960s and 1970s encouraged offshore drilling. This platform, which lies about 150 miles from Aberdeen, is both home and work station to roughly 100 people.

Photo by Bettmann/Hulton

Graffiti announces support for the home-rule movement, which favors giving Scotland its own legislature. Although backing for the idea has wavered, home rule continues to be a major issue among Scottish voters. Opinion polls suggest that four out of five Scots want their country to have some form of independence within a British state.

followed, and the ruling Labour party's majority in Scotland began to weaken.

In 1979 the Labour government offered Scotland its own assembly, authorizing a public vote to accept or reject this proposal. Although a majority of those voting approved of a Scottish legislature, not enough Scots participated in the vote.

A few months after this vote, Britain held national elections. The Labour party lost to the Conservatives, headed by Margaret Thatcher. Scotland, however, gave most of its support to Labour candidates in that election and in the national elections of 1983 and 1987. In 1995 Scotland had 49 Labour members of Parliament, 12 from other parties, and 11 from the Conservative party.

In recent years, national support for the Conservative party has decreased. The Labour party's plan for devolution of centralized British government, giving local governments more power, is still popular among Scots, but their vote in opinion polls is generally split between devolution and complete independence

Despite this problem, economic considerations are uppermost in the minds of most Scots. Although the oil finds have fostered employment in the east, the area around Glasgow has continued to decline. Since 1987 Scotland's economic growth as topped that of Britain as a whole and was less affected by the economic recession in the early 1990s. While Scots believe they would do well under home rule, their goal remains to achieve a good standard of living for the Scottish people.

Government

Under the terms of the Act of Union of 1707, Scotland retained its own legal system but gave up its separate parliament. Symbolically headed by a monarch, the United Kingdom is governed by the British Parliament and by a cabinet made up of members of Parliament (MPs). The prime minister is the most powerful person in the national government.

The British Parliament has two parts. The democratically elected House of Commons is more important than the hereditary House of Lords. The Commons has members from England, Scotland, Wales, and Northern Ireland. The House of Commons has 72 MPs from Scotland out of a total of 650 delegates. The Scottish Grand Committee, to which all Scottish MPs belong, considers bills that apply only to their country. When appropriate, separate acts of Parliament are passed to address special circumstances that exist in Scotland.

Scotland's judicial branch is distinct from that of England and Wales. The Scottish legal system is based on Roman civil law, rather than on English common law. This tradition means that legal decisions in Scotland reflect previous legislation instead of local custom. The Lord Advocate, Scotland's highest judicial officer, hears important criminal cases in the High Court. Sheriff courts and district courts make decisions in less serious cases. When rulings are in dispute, cases from these lower courts can be appealed to the Lord Advocate.

For administrative purposes, Scotland is divided into nine regions and three island areas. Each has its own elected council, which works with the Scottish Office in Edinburgh. The secretary of state for Scotland, who is a member of the national cabinet, heads the Scottish Office. The secretary has broad powers relating to agriculture, fisheries, education, health, housing, and roads.

Holyroodhouse is the official residence in Scotland of the British monarch. Although possessing only ceremonial power, the monarch is a symbol of unity for the four countries within the United Kingdom.

Photo by Ethel K. MacNeal

Hebridean fishermen pull in their nets at Stornoway, a port on the eastern coast of the island of Lewis. For many inhabitants of the Western Isles, fishing is still a major livelihood.

3) The People

More than 5 million people live in Scotland, out of a total of 58.6 million inhabitants in the United Kingdom. Roughly 75 percent of Scotland's population dwell in the Central Lowlands. The Highlands and the Southern Uplands are sparsely settled. Only a few thousand Scottish citizens make their homes in the outlying island areas.

Most Scots reside in cities and work in the manufacturing and service sectors of the economy. In rural areas, farming and herding are common occupations. Since the eighteenth century, emigration has remained steady as Scots leave in search of better job opportunities.

Ethnic Identity and Way of Life

Most Scottish people are descendants of the various European groups—including Celts, Vikings, Normans, and English—that invaded and settled the country. Scotland contains visual reminders of these peoples, ranging from Viking place names to Norman-style churches.

Age-old cultural differences remain between Highlanders and Lowlanders and

Highland games—which include dancing, music, and sports—offer opportunities for many Scots to take pride in their ties to the ancient clans.

between people from the Scottish mainland and people from the island areas. Orcadians, Shetlanders, and Hebrideans, for example, take pride in their Celtic and Viking ancestry and traditions.

Despite these variations, some common ground exists among Scots. The custom of drinking tea in the late afternoon occurs in villages and cities throughout Scotland. In the evenings, people from all walks of life visit local public houses (pubs) for refreshment, meals, and conversation. Many others watch television programs developed by independent stations or by the state-owned British Broadcasting Corporation.

Although the influence of the clans has declined, they still hold an important place in Scottish culture. Members wear traditional plaid kilts (pleated skirts) and listen to bagpipe music on ceremonial occasions. Each clan has its own plaid, called a tartan, which both men and women can display to symbolize their connection to a clan. A high proportion of Scots have last names beginning with "Mac" or "Mc"—a further tie to the ancient clans.

Language and Religion

English is Scotland's official language. The dialect of English spoken in the country is called Lallans or Scots. A whirring sound—known as a Scottish burr—is an identifiable feature of Scots, especially in words that contain the letter *r*. Rooted in the Anglo-Saxon tongue once used in northern England, Lallans also shows Gaelic and Viking influences.

Woolen mills throughout Scotland produce the plaid fabric used to make kilts and other goods. Each clan has its own tartan (plaid), which distinguishes one clan from another.

Courtesy of Minneapolis Public Library and Information Center

Along the southern Scottish border, a sign urges people leaving the country to hurry back.

The traditional language of Scotland is Scottish Gaelic. Similar to Irish Gaelic, this language developed when Celts from Ireland settled in the west and north in the late fifth century. As contact with Vikings, Anglo-Saxons, Normans, and English increased, however, the use of Scottish Gaelic declined.

In modern times, about 80,000 Scots speak Gaelic as a second language. Most of them live in the Highlands or on the outlying islands. The people in these areas make efforts to maintain their two-language culture by teaching and performing in Gaelic. The government encourages people to learn Gaelic language and culture through education, and by funding Gaelic organizations and television broadcasting.

The Church of Scotland, or Presbyterian Church, had a hand in the decline of Gaelic. In previous centuries, the church decided that English was the language best suited to spreading the faith. Although Scottish scholars translated the Bible into Gaelic and composed hymns in it, preaching and teaching were done in English.

The Church of Scotland, which now has about one million members, became the country's official religious organization in 1690. The Presbyterian belief system em-

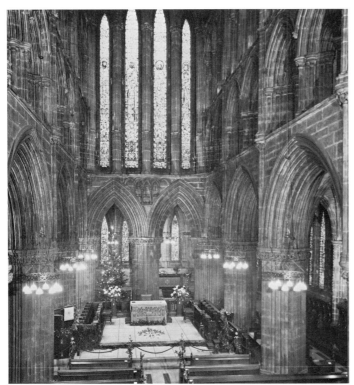

Begun in the 1200s, Glasgow Cathedral was built as a Roman Catholic place of worship. It now serves as the parish _kirk_ (church) of Glasgow, and its services follow the Presbyterian rites of the Church of Scotland. The cathedral is one of the best-preserved early buildings in the country.

Independent Picture Service

phasizes the equality of all of its followers. Elected representatives run the Church of Scotland, and both men and women can serve as ministers. The highest governing body of the church is the General Assembly. It meets annually in Edinburgh to discuss issues of religious, national, and worldwide importance.

Despite the existence of a state church, laws guarantee freedom of religion in Scotland. Small congregations of Baptists, Anglicans, Methodists, and Roman Catholics exist throughout the country.

Education, Health, and Welfare

Scotland's public educational traditions date to the 1400s, when the country's first universities were founded. In succeeding centuries, the Church of Scotland strongly emphasized schooling at the primary and secondary levels. By the early 1900s—despite the government's neglect of the

Independent Picture Service

Founded in 1451, the University of Glasgow once held classes in a crypt (burial chamber). Since the 1870s, the school has been at its present location, where roughly 10,000 students take courses in a variety of academic fields.

Art students make a chalk drawing in Glasgow's main outdoor mall to earn money for their schooling.

Courtesy of Sonya Olsen

45

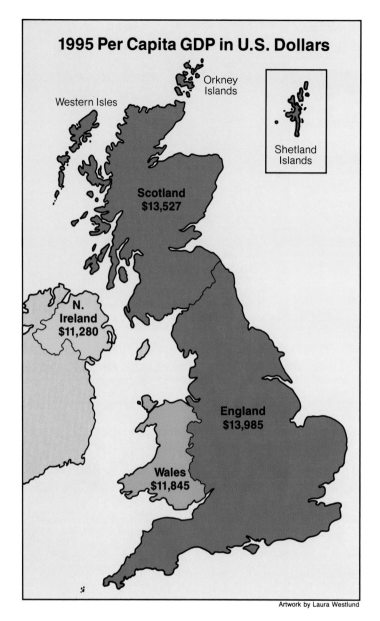

1995 Per Capita GDP in U.S. Dollars

Western Isles

Orkney Islands

Shetland Islands

Scotland
$13,527

N. Ireland
$11,280

England
$13,985

Wales
$11,845

Artwork by Laura Westlund

This map compares the average productivity per person—calculated by gross domestic product (GDP) per capita—for the four countries that make up the United Kingdom. The GDP is the value of all goods and services produced within the borders of each country in a year. To arrive at the GDP per capita, each country's total GDP is divided by its population. The resulting dollar amounts indicate one measure of the quality of life in Britain. The overall GDP figure for the United Kingdom is $13,762, but Scotland's amount is slightly lower. The difference may result from the slowing down of some of Scotland's traditional industries, such as coal mining and shipbuilding. Free medical care and other welfare services give most Scots a good standard of living. (Data taken from *Britain 1995,* prepared by the Central Office of Information.)

educational system—Scottish children were among the best educated youth in the United Kingdom.

In modern times, Scotland still operates its educational system separately from the rest of the United Kingdom. Recently, Scotland established school boards to oversee local educational facilities. The members include parents, teachers, and community leaders. The purpose of the boards is to increase parental and community involvement in education.

Most Scottish schools are government funded and teach boys and girls together. Children between the ages of 5 and 12 attend primary school. A six-year course follows at the secondary level. Well over 95 percent of the Scottish population can read and write. In secondary schools, courses focus on skills that prepare students for the job market. Mathematics, science, technical training, and English are typical subjects at this level.

After finishing secondary school, Scottish students have a variety of options. If the graduates qualify, they can choose to attend one of Scotland's 12 universities, which include St. Andrews, Glasgow, and Aberdeen. The students can also go to the many vocational schools throughout the country. The Open University is another educational choice. Founded in 1969, the Open University has no regular campus and offers its courses on television, on radio, on video cassettes, and through the mail.

Since 1945, Scotland has been part of a welfare state—that is, a nation where the government provides for the well-being of all of its citizens. A major part of this effort is the National Health Service, which supplies medical services at minimal cost to patients. This comprehensive program has brought many diseases under control.

The National Health Service has also helped to lower the number of Scottish infants who die within the first year of life. At 9 deaths per 1,000 live births, the rate is among the lowest in the world. The average life expectancy for a Scot is 74. The main causes of death are heart disease, stroke, and cancer.

The welfare state also gives funds to the elderly, the sick, the disabled, the unemployed, and widows. Welfare expenses have risen dramatically in recent years because of high unemployment. Some Scots, particularly youth from large urban centers, spend years living off their welfare checks—a situation called "being on the dole."

Wearing their academic robes, three students chat outside one of the buildings at the University of St. Andrews, Scotland's first institution of higher learning.

In a village near St. Andrews, a Scottish fisherman shows off a pair of fresh lobsters. Because of improved medical care, Scots have an average life expectancy of 74.

Literature and Music

Early Scottish literature focused on storytelling, in which bards (singer-poets) chronicled historical events and legends. Between the 1300s and 1500s, court poets, such as John Barbour and William Dunbar, contributed their written works to Scotland's literature. In the 1700s, the poet Allan Ramsey described rural life in Scotland, set old Scottish songs to new melodies, and founded the country's first public library.

Robert Burns—Scotland's most famous poet—was born in 1759 on a farm in southwestern Scotland. This background linked him to rural people, who continue to regard him as a national hero. Burns wrote in Scots and popularized the use of this dialect in England as well as in his homeland. He built his reputation on poetry and songwriting, and his first collection of poems, entitled *Poems, Chiefly in the Scottish Dialect*, was an immediate success.

Courtesy of Library of Congress

Born in rural Scotland, the poet and songwriter Robert Burns had a good ear for the use of the Scots language in verse and lyrics. After his death at the age of 37, he became a larger-than-life figure for many Scots, who valued his views on freedom, love, and nature.

Courtesy of Library of Congress

In the 1770s, Adam Smith put forward an economic theory that advised against governmental interference in free trade. Accepted by many British and U.S. businesspeople and politicians, Smith's theory has become a cornerstone of modern economic ideas.

Courtesy of Library of Congress

The works of the eighteenth-century thinker David Hume were widely criticized during his lifetime. In the nineteenth century, however, his scientific, political, and religious writings found an appreciative readership.

The novelist and poet Walter Scott often used events in Scotland's history as the setting for his stories and verse. He brought a keen sensitivity to his writings and introduced many British citizens to his country's stormy past.

In the 1700s and 1800s, Scotland produced many notable prose writers. The essayists Thomas Carlyle and David Hume broadened thinking on important political issues. Adam Smith wrote *The Wealth of Nations*, which has become a classic work of economic theory. The noted biographer James Boswell produced *Life of Samuel Johnson*. It gives a detailed account of the English scholar who compiled the first comprehensive English dictionary.

In this same period, Walter Scott and Robert Louis Stevenson entertained their readers with tales of adventure and romance. Scott's novels often dealt with events in Scotland's history. *Waverly* and *Rob Roy*, for example, are set during the Jacobite period. Another book, *Ivanhoe*, covers the exploits of a knight in the late twelfth century. Stevenson's most famous books are popular tales of adventure. *Kidnapped* involves secrecy in the Highlands, and *Treasure Island* is a story about piracy on the high seas. His short story, *The Strange Case of Dr. Jekyll and Mr. Hyde*, focuses on the darker side of human nature.

The well-known detective Sherlock Holmes was the creation of another Scot, Arthur Conan Doyle, who wrote his famous mysteries in the late 1800s and early 1900s. In the same period, J. M. Barrie produced the play *Peter Pan* and other children's stories.

As a child, Robert Louis Stevenson was often ill, and his health eventually forced him to live away from Scotland's wet climate. Although he is most famous for his adventure novels, Stevenson also produced many travel books.

J. M. Barrie based his play *Peter Pan* on the friendship he enjoyed with the five sons of a close friend. Barrie created a make-believe place, called Never-Never-Never Land, where pirates, Indians, boys, and fairies played, fought, and tricked one another. Here, the boys listen to a bedtime story.

Wearing kilts and feather bonnets, Scottish bagpipers play during a parade. They squeeze the bags as they blow into the pipes, producing a high-pitched sound.

Modern Scottish literature is diverse, ranging from the moving poetry of Hugh MacDiarmid to the tense thrillers of John Buchan. Like Burns, MacDiarmid used the Scots dialect but wrote some of his later works in traditional English. Buchan's detective, Richard Hannay, appeared in several novels, including *The Thirty-Nine Steps*, which became a movie.

Music has long been a vital part of Scotland's culture. The country's most familiar instrument is the bagpipe. This ancient wind instrument consists of a leather bag, often covered with a tartan, into which several pipes are inserted. The player blows into one pipe and, by pressing the bag,

forces air into the other pipes. The resulting sound can be shrill and sad. Bagpipe music is a major feature of Scottish parades, such as the Edinburgh Military Tattoo, and of traditional highland gatherings. The instrument often accompanies dances and marches.

Food

The rugged terrain of Scotland has limited farming mostly to the raising of livestock. As a result, traditional Scottish meals tend to be simple and filling. The national dish of Scotland is *haggis*, which combines various organs of a sheep or calf with

On January 25, the birthday of Robert Burns, diners gather in honor of the poet. The main part of the supper is *haggis,* a sausage-like dish that is often ceremonially presented as someone recites Burns's poem "Address to a Haggis."

51

A worker packs kippered (cured) herrings for transport. After they are caught, the fish are split and placed in salty water. They are then hung on long, horizontal poles in a smokehouse, where the smoke, wood, and fish oil give the herrings a special taste.

oatmeal and spices. This mixture is then stuffed into a casing made from a sheep's stomach and boiled. Honored by Robert Burns, this sausage-like meal is enjoyed throughout the country, especially on Burns Night (January 25), when groups gather in memory of the poet.

Soups, such as cock-a-leekie and Scotch broth, are filled with vegetables and meat. Fish dishes range from breakfast herrings called kippers to delicately smoked salmon from Scottish rivers. The country's well-known Aberdeen Angus cattle and Blackface sheep provide superior beef and lamb for Scottish tables.

Sports

Scots enjoy a wide variety of sports, both as participants and spectators. The most popular amateur team activity in Scotland is association football (soccer). Professional teams belong to the Scottish Football League, and their matches generate a lot of excitement. Rugby, from which U.S.

Each year, toughened competitors tramp through the rain and mud on a grueling race up Ben Nevis.

52

football is derived, is also a favorite spectator sport.

Golf originated in Scotland and has since become its most famous athletic activity. Also called the Royal and Ancient Game, golf is played throughout the country on small courses and at elite clubs. One of the world's most important golf tournaments, the British Open Championship, takes place annually at the Royal and Ancient Golf Club in the city of St. Andrews on the eastern coast.

Other sports in Scotland are seasonal. The country's scenic lakes and fast-flowing rivers attract fishing enthusiasts who come in search of salmon and trout. Downhill skiing has become increasingly popular since facilities in the Cairngorms and Glencoe were upgraded. The country's rugged terrain draws hikers and mountain climbers, especially to the region around Ben Nevis.

Highland games—traditional clan gatherings—are annual events. They bring out skilled athletes who can toss the caber (a heavy log), put the weight (shot put), or throw the hammer. Each September, the Royal Highland Gathering at Braemar attracts large crowds, as well as members of the British royal family.

At the annual Royal Highland Gathering at Braemar, a kilted athlete *(above)*, throws the hammer while Scotland's rugged terrain offers a rock climber *(left)* a different sort of challenge.

53

Off the coast of the Shetlands, gas flares from the Murchison oil field. Output from Britain's North Sea platforms reached 2.06 million barrels a day in the mid-1990s, making the nation one of the world's top 10 producers.

4) The Economy

As part of the United Kingdom, Scotland participates in an economy that is dependent on trade and manufacturing. In previous centuries, Scotland helped to make Britain the world's largest trading nation. By the mid-1930s, however, the industries and cities of Scotland had declined. Unemployment had risen to as high as 60 percent, and many people had left the country.

In the late 1960s and the 1970s, the economy revived when drilling rigs in Scotland's sector of the North Sea began to produce petroleum and natural gas. These deposits are still being tapped, and government efforts have improved some of the manufacturing areas. Through the Scottish Development Agency, foreign companies have set up branches in Scotland. These firms make electronics, research new technologies, and promote financial services.

Nevertheless, Scotland's overall economic outlook is still uncertain. Prices for the country's fossil fuels (coal, oil, and natural gas) vary with world market trends. Other nations are competing with Scotland for valuable foreign contracts, and investments have slowed. Unemployment has steadied at about 9.2 percent, and inflation, which measures changes in the average price of goods, is declining since the 1990 recession.

Bright lights shine from the buildings of a computer firm in Glasgow. Office equipment has become one of Scotland's main manufactured items.

Courtesy of Scottish Development Agency

Manufacturing and Mining

Most of Scotland's manufacturing plants are located in the Central Lowlands, although Aberdeen is the center of petroleum-related industries. Chemicals, sophisticated electronics, steel, textiles, and whisky head Scotland's list of manufactured items.

The country produces more than half of all the complex electronic equipment used in the United Kingdom and about 20 percent of the computers in operation on the European continent. Several microcomputer companies have branches in central Scotland, causing the strip between East Kilbride and Irvine to be nicknamed "Silicon Glen" after California's famous "Silicon Valley." (Silicon is one of the materials used to make computer microchips.)

Textiles, especially fine-quality yarns and wool fabrics, continue to be a mainstay of the Scottish economy. Traditional tweeds and sweaters made of wool from Hebridean and Shetland sheep have remained internationally popular. Yarn, rope, and carpets made of jute are still produced in Dundee, as are fine jams and computers.

Scotland's distilling industry also has a worldwide reputation. More than 80 percent of the country's whisky—called Scotch—goes to the United States. The industry uses locally grown barley and Scotland's own spring water to make the various whiskies, some of which are combined to produce special blends. Most of the distilleries are in eastern Scotland.

The whisky profits, however, do not all go to Scotland. Some large international corporations have taken over parts of the production process. Smaller, independent distillers are forced to seek out a larger partner for financial help. Glenfiddich remains an exception as a profitable, privately run distillery.

Courtesy of British Tourist Authority

At the Glenfiddich whisky distillery, new equipment, large vats, and careful quality control ensure a consistent product. Scotland's whisky industry has been active for nearly 200 years.

Once a thriving industry, coal mining in Scotland has steadily declined since the 1950s. Although workers still unearth coal in central Scotland, the country has become an overall importer of this mineral. Most of the coal fuels electric power stations in Scotland. In addition to coal, mines provide substantial quantities of silica sand, the raw material for glass.

Oil and Natural Gas

In the early 1960s, Scotland's economy was declining until deposits of petroleum and natural gas were found. By 1980 Britain had become self-sufficient in these fuels, and Scotland's financial situation had improved. The United Kingdom is now one of the top 10 oil-producing nations. Oil experts believe that Britain is approaching maximum production from its oil and gas resources. Nevertheless, the stocks should last well into the twenty-first century.

Drilling platforms now dot Britain's sector of the stormy North Sea. Work opportunities in eastern Scotland have multiplied, providing about 100,000 jobs for local inhabitants as well as for people from outside Scotland. There have been dangers, too. Explosions on the oil rigs, crashes of aircraft that bring workers to the rigs, and drownings of divers who check equipment have claimed many lives.

The main oil fields—including Brent, Forties, Kittiwake, and Ninian—lie near the Shetlands and the Orkneys. Pipelines and some tankers transport the crude oil to terminals at Sullom Voe, Flotta on the Orkneys, and Cruden Bay on the mainland. A large refinery exists at Grangemouth in east central Scotland.

The Killoch Colliery (coal mine) lies in central Scotland. Previously a state-run industry, many collieries have become privately managed in the 1990s.

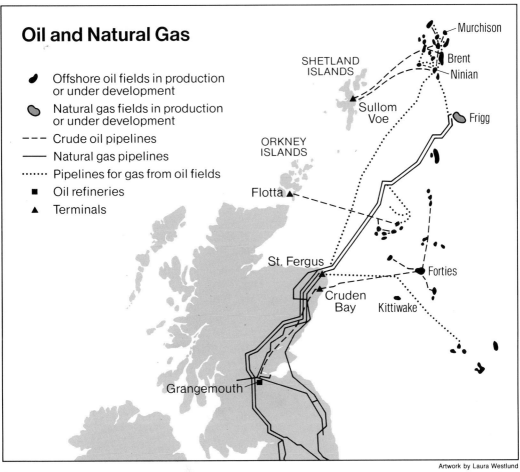

Oil and Natural Gas

🌢 Offshore oil fields in production or under development

🫘 Natural gas fields in production or under development

--- Crude oil pipelines

— Natural gas pipelines

...... Pipelines for gas from oil fields

■ Oil refineries

▲ Terminals

Murchison
SHETLAND ISLANDS
Brent
Ninian
Sullom Voe
Frigg
ORKNEY ISLANDS
Flotta
St. Fergus
Forties
Cruden Bay
Kittiwake
Grangemouth

Artwork by Laura Westlund

Most of Scotland's offshore oil fields also provide natural gas. Pipelines carry the crude oil and gas to the mainland, where refineries and terminals do further processing and transporting.

Natural gas from offshore sources erased Britain's need to import this fuel. Gas from the Norwegian-owned Frigg field, as well as gas by-products from British oil fields, is piped to a terminal at St. Fergus in the Highlands. Requiring less processing than crude oil, the gas goes from St. Fergus to homes and industries.

Agriculture and Fishing

About 80 percent of Scotland's land is used for agriculture. Farmers plant one-fourth of this amount with crops and devote the remainder to pasture. As a result, livestock dominates the agricul-tural sector. Dairy cattle are raised in the southwest lowlands, and beef cattle predominate in the northeast. Scottish cattle breeds include the Aberdeen Angus and the Galloway. Sheep, mostly of the Blackface variety, feed on rough grasses throughout the country.

In addition to these animals, Scottish breeders raise strong, load-pulling horses called Clydesdales. Another type, which originated on the Shetlands, is the Shetland pony—a small but sturdy horse. Because sheep raising has been so important to Scotland's economy, unique dog species were developed to guide the flocks. The collie originated in Scotland in the

Almost 50 percent of Scotland's land is devoted to raising livestock. Popular breeds include the Aberdeen Angus, the Galloway, and the West Highland.

On Harris, the southern section of the Hebridean island of Lewis, a sheep shearer shaves wool from one of his animals. The thick hair will probably become Harris Tweed—a rough woolen fabric used to make suits and coats.

1600s, and the Shetland sheepdog was specially bred to police the herds on the Shetlands.

Crop farming in Scotland concentrates on cereals, and until the 1960s oats were the country's main grain. Since then, barley has become the dominant crop because it brings higher yields and is more nutritious for livestock. In addition, barley provides an important ingredient to the distilling industry. Some oats and wheat are still grown in Scotland, along with small amounts of potatoes and turnips. Sections of east central Scotland produce raspberries, meeting 85 percent of the national demand.

Fishing is a centuries-old occupation in Scotland, and about 75 percent of the entire British catch arrives in Scottish fishing ports. This livelihood is changing rapidly, as new nets, better technology, and bigger boats make fishing more effi-

cient. But improvements in equipment have also led to overfishing and shortages. Since 1977 a ban has existed on most large-scale herring fishing in the North

Small piles of grain dot the landscape of the Orkneys, where the soil is fertile enough to grow some crops.

Sea. The European Union Fisheries Policy now limits the amount of fish to be caught per year in order to avoid shortages in other fish populations.

Whitefish have since dominated Scotland's catch, and Peterhead on the country's eastern coast is the leading whitefish port in Europe. Fleets of trawlers operate from Peterhead, Aberdeen, Lerwick, and Fraserburgh in search of cod, haddock, mackerel, and whiting. Fishing crews also land hauls of lobster, shrimp, and crab from the cold waters.

With natural supplies declining, fish farming has increased in Scotland. The industry, which receives development funds from the government, raises rainbow trout and Atlantic salmon in specially monitored tanks and ponds.

Transportation and Energy

Overall, Scotland has good road, railway, and air-transportation systems. In some northern and eastern areas of the country, however, roads and services are limited. About 55,000 miles of paved roads crisscross Scotland, including modern highways that connect Glasgow and Edinburgh. These cities also have good overland links to London. Routes in the north are usually of poorer quality, and the roads in the west and on some islands can be rough and narrow.

Scotland's railways link Glasgow and Edinburgh to each other and to London. The comfortable intercity trains from London to Glasgow run at very high speeds, while those to Edinburgh take longer because of many stops along the route. Glasgow also has its own underground train system, which brings people to destinations throughout the city. The islands and some of mainland Scotland's remote areas have no train services.

Ferries and airlines operate between the mainland and the islands. In the oil-producing areas, travel by air has become

Shetland fishermen remove their catch of salmon from nets at Uyeasound, Unst.

very common. Helicopters bring crews of workers from the Shetlands and the Orkneys to the drilling platforms. Domestic and European airlines fly into the airports at Glasgow, Edinburgh, and Aberdeen. The field at Prestwick, near Glasgow, mostly receives transatlantic traffic.

Because of oil activities, some of Scotland's ports are thriving. Sullom Voe, built on an abandoned military base, handles more than 50 million tons of cargo each year. Within Britain, only London has a greater volume of shipping. The docks at Hunterston (on the Clyde), Grangemouth, Flotta, and Aberdeen are also busy year-round.

Scotland has abundant energy sources. The country contains the largest hydropower facilities in the United Kingdom. Many rivers and streams have been dammed to provide electricity to Scotland and northern England. Two state-owned boards share the job of operating the country's hydropower facilities in Fasnakyle, Rannoch, Lochay, Cruachan, and Clunie.

The express train known as The Flying Scotsman first took to the track in 1862, covering the distance between London, England, and Edinburgh in 10.5 hours. With the addition of modern engines, the trip now takes less time.

Independent Picture Service

The nuclear power station at Chapelcross became operational in the late 1950s. About 40 percent of the country's electrical power comes from nuclear sources.

Independent Picture Service

Led by its owner, a donkey laden with blocks of peat makes its way up a narrow road. In remote areas, people still rely on dried peat, which burns like wood, for fuel.

Photo by Ethel K. MacNeal

Anglers try their luck on the Tweed River in southern Scotland.

Independent Picture Service

Nuclear plants, which provide about 40 percent of Scotland's electricity, exist at Hunterston and Chapelcross. Oil-fueled and coal-fired power stations are located at Peterhead and Inverkip. Dried peat—decayed vegetation that can be burned as fuel—is often used to heat homes in remote areas of the Highlands and on the islands.

Trade and Tourism

As part of the United Kingdom, Scotland participates in an active trading economy.

The country's main exports are electronic equipment, petroleum, chemicals, textiles, and whisky. Most of these products go to buyers in Europe and North America. Scotland's major imports include food, machinery, and vehicles. European nations, the United States, and Japan are the most active suppliers of Scotland's imports.

Tourism is also an important industry in Scotland, earning more than $3 billion annually and providing 180,000 jobs. With its beautiful, largely unspoiled scenery, the country attracts both domestic and international traffic. People from Glasgow and

Standing at the northern end of Loch Awe, Kilchurn Castle is a romantic, much-visited ruin that once belonged to the Campbell clan.

Walkers and Shetland sheep scamper along the rocky, green hillsides of Unst.

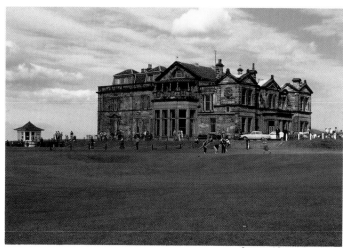

The clubhouse of the Royal and Ancient Golf Club at St. Andrews overlooks the "Old Course," where golfers from all over the world come to play.

Massed bands of bagpipers are featured in the annual Edinburgh Military Tattoo (evening entertainment by soldiers). The spectacle, which is part of the Edinburgh International Festival, takes place just beyond the walls of Edinburgh Castle.

Edinburgh leave their urban surroundings for the scenic lochs that dot the countryside. Fishing enthusiasts come to the unpolluted rivers and lakes in search of salmon and trout. Adventuresome hikers tackle Scotland's rugged terrain.

As many as 10 million foreign visitors, some of them of Scottish descent, arrive each year to experience the distinctive culture of Scotland's highland clans. They also travel to the country's many famous golf courses, including St. Andrews, Gleneagles, and Turnberry. Glasgow's fine art museums, especially the Burrell Collection, are major attractions. Annual events, such as the Edinburgh International Festival and the Royal Highland Gathering at Braemar, also draw many people to Scotland.

The Future

In the 1970s and 1980s, Scotland began to recover from a long period of economic decline. With foreign investments, the coun-try broadened its manufacturing base to include sophisticated electronic items, such as computer hardware. With government funds, Scotland attempted to rehabilitate its traditional industries. The nation's oil income, however, benefits the United Kingdom, not just Scotland. Some Scottish people object to this arrangement, and slogans proclaiming "It's Scotland's Oil" have appeared on buildings and signs throughout the country.

Some Scots are content with the union with England. Other citizens want more self-rule for Scotland. Institutions such as the Church of Scotland and the Scottish legal system have helped the country to maintain an identity separate from the rest of Britain. But strong health and welfare programs have resulted from Scotland's ties to the United Kingdom. By balancing the advantages of being both Scottish and British, Scotland's people may share in Britain's economic and social progress while shaping it to meet Scottish goals.

Index